The Other Side of
UNFORGIVENESS

Your Guide to Overcoming Personal Hurt

ACCLAIM

"Based on Danita Lynne's personal experiences, *The Other Side of Unforgiveness* is an insightful and compelling read. There are many truths to the principles in her story, and I found myself relating to some of the reasons why forgiveness has not been an option."

Deanna Johnson
Educator

"*The Other Side of Unforgiveness* is a riveting new book by Danita Lynne! Alive with the accounts of choice and consequence, Danita Lynne guides the reader past the pain of yesterday...and possibly today, and into the possibilities of tomorrow. Acceptance is the first step – My name is Dr. Pamela Collins and I am headed to the other side."

Pamela Collins, Ph.D.
Assistant Professor

"Danita Lynne's recounting of her journey to forgiveness is a powerful and compelling story. The beginning chapter alone is provocative, pointed, and impacting. Reading it brought to mind several instances of my own experiences that I realized I wanted to let go of and give forgiveness to those involved. I have already planned to share this book with several friends and family members as a great gift!"

Antonio Goodwin
Author, *The Interpreted Life*

"Wow! Anyone can find themselves in one of the scenarios in this book. The crutch analogy was the perfect visual for me in areas of unforgiveness I have been operating in. I have to learn to walk without it as I don't need it anymore."

Amber Z. Middleton, M.Ed., M.S., Ed.S
Education Director

"What comes to mind when you hear the word *Unforgiveness*? Whatever it is, it probably won't be the same after you read this road-map to healing, self-improvement, and the power of releasing "self" from emotional and mental captivity. This enlightening, and sometimes shocking, debut work from Danita Lynne cements her place amongst the self-help authors of this century.

Human beings are complex multi-dimensional beings, as such Danita takes the time to lay a foundation for readers to "do the work" necessary to look within and take ownership. Her story can easily be a part of the intricately woven tapestry of womanhood, but it digs deep into the lived human experience. It constantly challenges the reader to look at how the choice not to forgive can have a detrimental impact on one's life."

Catrell Harris, MPH

"This book is certain to be an effective resource in aiding many to overcome pain, disappointment, and discombobulation that will most likely present itself to everyone at some point in their lifetime. Danita Lynne gives practical tools that will assist you to rise above the offense and proceed to a place of calmness, wholeness, and strength, to obtain a fresh start."

Deborah Grant

Associate Pastor

Spirit of Faith Christian Center Ministries

"*The Other Side of Unforgiveness* has the potential to evoke unhealthy and unhealed emotions, which is a good thing, and not without offering the reader multiple solutions to experience intentional, emotional healing. Danita Lynne's narrative is heartbreaking, yet I was compelled to continue to read her story as if I were on the sidelines cheering her on for the successful completion of her "personal marathon" towards forgiveness."

LaShawn Demery
Leading Lady, BIBLEWAY Church of Washington, DC

"Danita Lynne has written an incredible book about the power of forgiveness that I'm sure will inspire many people to do the work and become healed from past hurts and disappointments. The wisdom of her personal story is relevant and relatable, and she has broken down her concepts into practical applications that anyone can follow to start or continue along their forgiveness journey."

Jennifer Westbrook
JenWestWriting Editing & Marketing Services

The Other Side of
Unforgiveness

Your Guide to Overcoming Personal Hurt

DANITA LYNNE

ENGLISH & SIGN LANGUAGE MASTERS, LLC

The Other Side of Unforgiveness
Copyright ©2019 by Danita Lynne

Printed in the United States of America
First Printing, 2019
ISBN 978-1-7332527-0-6
Published by:
English & Sign Language Masters, LLC
Landover, MD
Danita.ESLM@gmail.com
www.theothersideofforgiveness.com

Cover Design: Sheikh Studios (PVT.) LTD.
Interior Design: Glory to Glory Publications, LLC
Editor: JenWestWriting Editing & Marketing Services
Back Cover Photo: Lindria Dockett Photography

This is a work of creative nonfiction. The events are of the author's life and experiences. All the stories in this book are true and told solely from the author's perspective. None of the recalled memories are in any way intended to defame any person, or place.

ACKNOWLEDGMENTS

Thank you, God, for showing me every day what forgiveness looks like, so I don't ever have to wonder. You continue to love me, bless me, and give me infinite chances to make right the things I have messed up, even though you give clear instructions. The feeling of knowing you still love me through all of this is what gives me the grace to forgive anything and the ability to guide others through the process as well.

Thank you, Aaron, for being the BEST SON EVER. When I prayed for a son, I asked God for the ability to be able to learn from you, no matter your age. Every day, as I meander through this thing called parenting and make mistakes, you love me through them and show me what forgiveness looks like. Learning to forgive others like I forgive you is one of the best things I ever learned. And learning to forgive others like you forgive them is just as amazing.

Thank you, Daddy and Mommie (Earl and Dottie Wheeler), for the relentless love and support you have given me through all of the ups and downs in my life. Your teaching always comes to me by example and I have learned to give and forgive, treat people right, and love without limits from you two. I am blessed beyond measure to have you in my life and in Aaron's life.

Thank you, Apostle Michael and Pastor Deloris Freeman, for teaching me faith like I have never been taught it before. When I decided to become an expert at forgiving, I use what I learned from you about faith to visualize what that looked like until what I wanted was realized. Now I am able to use this visualization method each time I need to get to the other side of unforgiveness.

Thank you, family and friends, both for making this book possible and sometimes, making it necessary. What can I say? We have made it through our struggles and learned to keep fighting to stay in each others' lives. That is how our relationships get stronger. I love you all. Let's keep using the principles in this book to love each other better so we can make this world better together.

Thank you, mentors and partners, who knowingly and unknowingly guided me, helped me, and pushed me to get this book finished. You have changed the course of my life for the better, forever.

And finally, thank you, readers, for buying this book, reading it, and putting into practice what you read. Don't be afraid to take your time and read it in segments because you may not be able to simultaneously apply all that you learn. It is my hope that you open your heart to receive all that you need to get to the other side of unforgiveness. Since this book is in your hand, you have already made a huge first step. Keep going. Keep growing.

"AS I WALKED OUT THE DOOR TOWARD THE
GATE THAT WOULD LEAD TO MY FREEDOM,
I KNEW IF I DIDN'T LEAVE MY BITTERNESS
AND HATRED BEHIND, I'D STILL BE IN PRISON."

NELSON MANDELA

Contents

"Oh, God! Where is the bottom! Where is the real honest-to-God bottom so he can't go any farther!"

Raisin in the Sun
Lorraine Hansberry

Introduction

This Had to Be the Bottom

I woke up at 4 AM with one plan in mind—to catch him at her house so that he could no longer deny it. I had seen signs that he was cheating for months now and even confronted him about it a few times, but he always denied it. He had denied everything from my questioning his typical "I'm working late" excuse to my inquiry about him sprinkling baby powder in the laundry basket to hide the scent of promiscuity on his clothes. I was no fool, but I was certainly being treated as one, and there is almost nothing I hate worse. By this time, I had even solicited the services of a private detective to track down my then-husband, only to be refused the services because the detective would not take my money. "When a woman suspects her man of cheating," he said, "there are only two things possible: she's paranoid, or she's right. You have to figure out which one you are." I knew I was right. Money saved. I had already found her number in his cell phone and looked her up online to match her highly-unique name to an address.

I drove an hour to her home that morning, parked out front, and called her house telephone number that I had found online. If there was any doubt whether or not I was in the right place, it was uncomfortably eased because the car he drove was parked there on the street...the car with my name on the registration. In a hazy, half-asleep voice, she answered, to which I replied, "Hello, this is Danita. I'm outside. Can you put my husband on the phone, please?" In seconds, I heard his voice. "Come out here now," I said in the calmest voice that I could muster. He hung up. After what was probably just a minute or so, I felt like he was taking too long to come outside, so I called again. This time, he answered. "If you don't want a scene in this neighborhood, I suggest you come outside NOW."

A few moments later, the front door cracked open, and he emerged. I got out of the car, and he approached me with the most ironic question I have ever been asked, "What are you doing here?" In my mind, I snatched him by the throat and said, "No, what are YOU doing here?" In real life, only the latter part happened. We had a verbal altercation that I couldn't recall if you paid me, but I know the whole thing ended with me trying to get his car keys out of his hand so that I could drive back home and leave him stranded. It didn't even matter how I was going to get the other car home. I would figure that out later. If he wanted to be there, then he could stay there, but not with access to my car. I don't even recall why I decided to leave, but I couldn't get the keys away from him, so I jumped into my car. I tried to at least run over his feet as I pulled off, but fortunately for him, he jumped back, and I sped down the street. I don't know if anyone else saw what happened that morning. I didn't care.

That was one of the lowest points in my life. My whole world had shattered, and the man I had married was to blame. He had picked up my fragile heart and slammed it to the ground, seemingly without regard for the impact it had on the woman he had promised to love "from this day forward, as long as [we] both shall live." Many depressing moments followed that horrific scene. In those moments, I made countless poor decisions, including holding on to my shattered marriage because I thought that staying married while believing things would improve was how I showed I had faith. That's another story.

Eventually, I had a revelation and filed for divorce. After that day in court when the divorce was finalized, it would be years later before I had to see him again. The untimely death of his father, whom I loved dearly, summoned my presence at the funeral service. Likewise, I wanted to go to support my dad, whose friendship with my ex-husband's father had been unphased by our breakup. Until the moment I saw my ex in the church's foyer, I was unsure how I would feel when I saw him again. I imagined several possibilities: I might want to hurt him physically; I might immediately retreat when I came face to face with him, or I might be delighted to learn of some deep level of suffering he had been enduring since our divorce. But I hoped that none of those would be true. I really just wanted confirmation that since I had completed a few weeks of therapy with a Christian counselor and had taken deliberate steps to relocate my self-confidence, I had truly healed. That's how I wanted to feel, but I was unsure if I would get what I wanted. After all, my record of getting what I wanted had not been great.

Even though this was a man that I had truly loved with all of my heart, our brief but tumultuous marriage had not even lasted past our first anniversary. Since ten months was far less than "until death do we part," if seeing him had revealed to me that I was still bitter, I would have felt justified. But the opposite happened. The man I saw was in anguish, and I opened my arms to give him a genuine hug filled only with consolation. I had healed. I had forgiven, and in that moment, I used my hug to convey all of that to him.

Back then, I didn't realize how unforgiveness took a person to a dark place. I had only realized that although not forgiving him would have been justified, it was not what I had been taught. My earthly father, the most forgiving man I know, taught me unconditional forgiveness. I've seen and heard about some of his worst experiences and know first-hand that none of those things have stayed with him. He lets everything go. It's amazing...but to an untrained forgiver, it can be maddening. But I wanted to be like that. And without realizing it, I had done it. Since then, I began to study patterns in life and pay attention to how people deal with hurtful situations. Quick to notice that people who forgive are ultimately happier people, I began calling myself a "master forgiver" because frankly, I prefer being happy. Sure, that sounds weird because it seems to imply that not everyone likes being happy. But guess what? If you make a habit of being unforgiving, you make a habit of being unhappy. It is just that simple.

And with that, I want to challenge you. I want you to read this book with an open heart. I want you to be honest with yourself about where you fit in the descriptions of feelings or emotions that keep you locked in unforgiveness. I want you to see what message you are really sending to yourself when you harbor unforgiveness. I want you to see what you are missing out on when you hold onto unforgiveness. I want you to take baby steps to accomplish everyday practices that can lead you to forgive anyone for anything. And most of all, I want you to start right now.

"YOUR WHOLE DESTINY COULD BE TIED UP IN
WHAT YOU WON'T DO."

STACIA PIERCE

ONE

I Can't Forgive Because...

C an't we always think of more than enough reasons not to do something that isn't easy? No matter how beneficial the goal is to us, thinking of a way out seems to come way too naturally for most of us. I can be totally disgusted with the way my clothes are fitting but still decide that because the previous day was so long, I need to sleep in rather than get up early enough to work out. You may be trying to improve your punctuality and have to be somewhere at a certain time, but because you know they started late the last time, you give yourself yet another timeliness pass because this one "doesn't count." You could know that no matter what you tell yourself, you still have not forgiven that person who hurt you in a way you did not even think was possible. You had safeguarded yourself against being hurt again and vowed no one would ever hurt you that way again. Yet it happened anyway...again. The mere idea of forgiving makes you feel vulnerable to the pain of every prior hurt. Forgiving again will only make you appear weak, and you will not stand for that. At least staying upset makes sense and keeps you in control of the situation. Or does it?

I recall when one of my mentors asked a tough question. He said, "Do you know that it's possible to fail for legitimate reasons?" I remember being so stuck on that question that I cannot even recall what he said after that for the next few minutes. It was like he had single-handedly wiped out any reason I could create for not being successful at something I wanted badly enough. So, let's apply that concept here. I know there are so many legitimate reasons why you can't seem to forgive whoever hurt you, but if it's ultimately keeping you from successfully moving forward in every area of your life, it has to be worth it to try harder. In this chapter, we will look at seven reasons you may be telling yourself you can't forgive and dissect them a bit. Approach this chapter fully aware that while there are seven reasons here, there are still only two possible results: forgiveness or unforgiveness. And there is a way to get to the other side of unforgiveness. You just have to understand the benefits of forgiveness enough to want them more than your current situation.

Reason #1- *It still hurts.* It really hurts, and because I know there is a wide variety of things that you could be hurting from, I am not at all trying to trivialize this. People do awful things, and the residual effects that they have on those who are hurt by them are often long-lasting. Someone could be perpetuating a lie that has you looking like a distorted version of yourself; you may have had a horrendous experience like having been assaulted or raped; you may have lost a loved one due to an accident or a crime where someone else was at fault. Whatever the situation, it can have you dealing with all kinds of raw feelings that impact your life in a way that changes your whole definition of "normal." Your life will never be the same, and the whole experience has left you feeling powerless because you cannot get back the untarnished reputation ruined by the lies told about you. You cannot regain the virginity the rapist stole from you; you cannot get back that loved one whose life is over because of someone else's negligence or reckless behavior. But here's the thing: those are all variables that you cannot control. The one variable that you can control is using your own power to forgive. Forgive anyway. You know why? Because holding unforgiveness is just a different kind of pain that you are adding to the pain of the hurt you are already enduring.

Think about it. When you are plagued with thoughts of what happened and how it hurt so bad, it brings with it a pain that is almost as real as it was the day it happened. After I confronted my then-husband at his girlfriend's house, I slipped into what I believe was a mild, undiagnosed depression. Now, I am completely unable to recall the details of any given day, but I know that after several months, I had effortlessly lost a significant amount of weight, slept most days, and lay awake most nights. I replayed that moment in my mind over and over, and I cried every time. Hard. I didn't realize it then, but now I see how every thought was like ripping the bandage off of a deep wound that was not healed all the way through, causing it to ooze and bleed all over again.

Think of forgiveness as if it were that bandage. When you choose unforgiveness, it's equivalent to leaving the wound exposed to anything that can get inside and cause infection, thus making the wound worse. However, when you decide that it is best to protect yourself with a bandage that will keep infection out of the wound, or at least reduce the chances of infection, it is another way of looking at your decision to get to the other side of unforgiveness and to protect yourself from further injury. Forgiveness is the bandage that swaddles you in the comfort of being free to move around more easily as you do the everyday work that soothes the hurt and keeps your heart in a peaceful place.

Reason #2-*The person doesn't deserve to be forgiven.* You are absolutely right. None of us deserves forgiveness. But that is not what this is about. At the very center of the word "forgiveness" is the word "give." Therefore, we must look at forgiveness as a gift to the person who has done something wrong. And if we made a habit of only giving things to people when they deserved them, very few of us would have all that we do because, at some point, we have received something based on need, not merit. Furthermore, we give things that represent who we are and not who the person is. Admit it. When the time comes to buy a gift for someone, you put thought into what the recipient, or anyone else, will think when they see the gift. You go out in search of the perfect gift, something so nice that you wouldn't mind keeping it for yourself, or that you are absolutely sure the recipient will enjoy because it just matches so person well. All of this is relevant because the gift you give is a reflection of you. It makes you look good. The same is true for forgiveness. Whether or not you think the person you have to forgive deserves it, being the one who forgives makes you look good. You show people that you are the bigger person, the one who "took the high road" and decided that it doesn't matter if the person deserves it or not.

More importantly, you must choose to forgive because no one will ever truly *deserve* it. Either you or someone you know has forgiven someone of something that caused the majority of people in your life to call you crazy for forgiving. You tolerated bad behavior that may have elicited a verbal apology, but at the same time, the person's actions did not show any remorse. Conversely, you may also be able to recall a time when the offender has done everything right to show a change in behavior, but for whatever reason, the forgiveness never fully happens. Either way, you can decide to forgive someone who doesn't seem to be working to earn your forgiveness just as easily as you can decide not to forgive someone who is trying hard to make things right with you. It is your choice to give it to whomever you want. You have the power.

Reason #3-*You don't want to.* As I just stated, the power to forgive is within you, so if you decide that you don't want to give it, that is a choice *and consequence* that you have to accept. Consider it this way: my mentor of over fifteen years, who is also my pastor, says all the time that "Your response is your responsibility.[1]" Let that sink in. You have no control over what someone does to you, but you do control your reaction to it. So, whether you believe in biblical principles, like "you reap what you sow," or general laws of the universe, like "what goes around comes around," you cannot go around quoting either and thinking it only applies to the person who committed the wrongdoing. Choosing unforgiveness positions you to receive the same treatment when the time comes for you to need some forgiveness of your own. And the time will come.

I am going to keep saying this: you have to decide to forgive. No one can make you want to or not want to. Part of the beauty of being human is having the gift of choice. You can choose to speak to your coworker or pretend you don't see her. You can let that person in traffic change over to your lane or drive as closely as possible to the car in front of you, so the merging driver can't get in. You can hold open the door to the store you are exiting for the person about to enter, or let it close and keep walking. But when you choose the latter of any of the options I just mentioned, you can miss finding out from your coworker that your morning meeting was just canceled, so you don't have to rush to leave your office. You can have an accident with the car in front of you because you were too close and weren't expecting that slow down to come to a full stop just yet. You can have the oncoming shopper think you are a total jerk. I am using minute examples to make a point that applies to any situation. You will have to deal with the consequences of your choices. Choosing to stay in a state of unforgiveness is a selfish behavior that hoards a gift you are supposed to give away. The other side of that is that you must be willing to accept that others, too, can decide not to forgive you if you hurt them.

Reason #4- *The person you need to forgive is deceased.* So, now you may be wondering how I could possibly tell you that you need to forgive a dead person. You do it the same way you do anything else regarding someone deceased. People visit grave sites to leave flowers, go to the scene of an accident where someone died to place stuffed animals, photos, and anything else memorable, and make posts on social media wishing a happy birthday to their loved one who is no longer with them. And do you know why people do all of those things? It helps them heal. This is the same reason why you have to figure out a way to forgive the person who hurt you, even if he or she isn't living. You need to heal, and the person does not need to be physically there for you to do it.

When I was going through my healing process with my ex-husband, he was not present. Sure, he was alive, but years had passed from the day our divorce was final to the day I saw him at his father's funeral. I did not suddenly decide to forgive him in that moment. It was only because I had already let go of unforgiveness that I was able to go there. I admit that I was unsure of how I would react to seeing him again, but that was just doubt creeping in, making me think I wasn't ready to face him. Still, I stuck to my decision and my feelings followed. Things could have been different. We did not have any children or property together, so after the divorce was final, we had no reason to stay in touch with one another. I only found out about his father's passing because our fathers were still friends. Even if that had not been the case, I still would have had to process all of my feelings and do the work of forgiving for my own sanity. I could not continue living the upside-down life I was living, or rather existing. It's true that I used the encounter at the funeral as a barometer to measure my level of forgiveness. But had I not gone, I still would have been able to gauge by my ability to think back on the marriage without being overcome with grief or anger anymore. By whatever means necessary, I would have figured it out. You can do the same. Do not allow the fact that someone is not physically accessible keep you from living the life of freedom that you want and need.

Reason #5- *You hate confrontation.* You have always been characterized as someone with a passive personality. You are the one who wants everyone to get along. You are the one who would rather suffer in silence than let the person who wronged you know what actually happened while he or she goes on with life, clueless that any wrongdoing occurred. You are the one who cannot stand the thought of getting into an uncomfortable conversation because it will only make matters worse. You are still dealing with the hurt, so in your mind, discussing it will only compound the injury. You are thinking that confronting the person is not going to help because it's clear she doesn't even care. Do any of these resonate with you?

Let's look at the word *confrontation*. How does it make you feel? What do you think of when you hear that word? For many, only negative thoughts arise when that word comes up, but that does not have to be the case. While I would not necessarily categorize myself as one who enjoys confrontation, I am indeed one who loves relationships, which includes confrontation. I believe that to enjoy a mutually beneficial relationship thoroughly, it's worthwhile to confront someone when it can lead to an even better relationship. I consider every interaction with a person as a relationship; some just last longer than others. These relationships can be with a colleague, someone in my family, a new friend, a long-time friend, a love interest, or the front desk clerk at the hotel. All of these are important to me, and if I need to confront any of these people regarding something that hinders our peaceful interaction, I do it.

I did not say all that to convince you to be like me. Some people probably hate that I so readily confront people. It can be too much at times. Still, I am encouraging you to look at confrontation as a positive rather than a negative act. When your goal is to confront someone to restore peace, a positive outcome is possible. With love as your motivation, you can diffuse the predisposed hostility because that love should come out in your word choice and tone. The look on your face or a soft touch, if appropriate, can usually bring someone who is usually defensive to a less hostile posture. If you are confronting a person who is fully aware of the wrong done to you, and even more so, how you feel about it, it can be confusing to see a loving approach coming from you. Use that confusion to your advantage and catch the person off-guard. Make it clear that although she hurt you, it is important for you to learn her perspective concerning the matter so that you can resolve the situation and lessen the likelihood of repeat offenses. This confrontation is not about proving her wrong and you right, but about getting to a better place in your future interactions.

Reason #6- *You like the attention.* Let's be real. You may just be so caught up in the saga of the "Poor you! I can't believe he did that to you!" show that you don't know how to let go of it all and move on. What's ironic is that in this scenario, you may not be as hurt as you have made yourself out to be, but because it actually feels good to finally have some attention on you, capitalizing on this moment seems reasonable to you. For the first time in a long time, or maybe the first time ever, people are calling to check on you to see how you are doing. You are enjoying the company of more friends than usual. You feel like people actually care about you. So in your own way, this hurtful incident is actually working in your favor—or at least you think it is.

In actuality, you are missing the truth of what is happening. You are reaping temporary benefits at someone else's expense. You may feel like it serves them right for what they did to you, but again, forgiving someone is about *you*. While you are convinced that wallowing in the victim role is okay for now, the additional time you allow this to play out only extends the time between when you transition from this pacifier—all the attention you have been getting—to the true healing where you do not need any of it. Think of it like a child who is quiet in class and never causes the teacher any problems, but she suddenly begins to misbehave because she notices that the teacher keeps unruly students in the classroom during recess. Since the child hates recess because the other kids pick on her, this is the perfect solution. She will take the attention however she can get it, even when it is avoiding the real problem that can only be resolved by addressing the children who tease her at recess. Like the girl in this scenario who chooses not to confront (there's that word again) her classmates to resolve the true issue, you are finding a place of comfort in the attention gained from anyone who caters to you instead of challenging you to handle the real problem.

Dependence on attention is holding you back, and you can be free from it. Think of it as an exchange. People will certainly be ready to give you attention if you stand up for yourself to address something wrong that was done to you. Especially if others don't typically see this kind of boldness from you, they will certainly be more attentive to you standing up for yourself because it will catch them off-guard. Your new approach to garnering attention will be a refreshing change. Give onlookers a positive reason to pay attention to you. This way, you are not going to lose attention altogether; you will just lose the attention that carries a negative aura with it.

Reason #7- *You don't know how.* For as long as you can recall, you may have heard the phrase "forgive and forget," as if the two actions are necessary equals. Some people will have you believe that if you cannot forget the wrong done to you, that you have not truly forgiven. I not only think that is crazy; I don't think it is possible. As humans, we remember how something made us feel long after we forget the details of what actually happened. This fact alone makes the pressure to combine forgiveness with forgetting a daunting task, at best. As a result, you may find yourself stuck or resolving that you just can't do it. It may feel like you have tried in the past to forgive the person, but it isn't working. Each time the person comes around, or someone mentions his name, you feel yourself getting angry or feeling sad all over again. Perhaps you could not really identify with any of the sentiments above because everything in you truly wants to forgive, but here you are, reading the same book on unforgiveness as everyone else because you realize that it is going to take more than what you have tried in the past to get to the other side of unforgiveness completely. It is going to take some work, and it won't be easy.

Let me help you. One of the hardest parts of doing the work of forgiveness is being consistent. It isn't that you don't know how to forgive; it is that you did not realize that it was not something that happens overnight. Later in the book, I will talk more in depth about how deciding to forgive is the first step in an ongoing process. But for now, let's focus on getting you to the realization that forgiveness may have actually worked if you had not given up on yourself so quickly.

While it sometimes only takes a moment to experience something extremely hurtful, let's agree that it takes more than a moment to recover from it. Calling upon my scenario with my ex again, I will emphasize that it took more occasions than I can count to notice that the pain from it all was possibly starting to subside. There were plenty of people who knew that I had gotten married but who also had not seen me since. And what's the natural question to ask someone who just got married? "How's married life treating you?" There it was. The dagger in my heart...being twisted by someone who thought she was asking an innocent question. My reply was always an indicator to me of my degree of forgiveness. As I ran into various people at various times who all asked their own variation of this same question, I noticed that my responses had transformed. Initially, my answer was full of rage while I tried to be polite at the same time. After all, it wasn't that person's fault that my marriage was over. She was just checking to see how I was doing. She was either happy I had joined the wives club, living vicariously through me while awaiting her own chance to be married too, or she was just happy because I was.

Either way, a woman who genuinely cared about me and meant no harm did not deserve to have my unforgiveness for my ex spewed onto her. Who was I to crush her happiness with my bitter answers? I was Wrong, with a capital W. I had to find a way to make my answers softer. I didn't realize that was how I was teaching myself to forgive truly. While I had committed to my decision to get divorced and move on, I was still angry. The harshness of my answer was evident all over the faces of anyone who inquired how married life was going for me. Seeing the hurt and shock they must have felt grieved me. It often appeared as if I was hurting their feelings because my feelings were hurt. So, I started preparing my answers in advance. I would practice responding in different tones of voice, making sure it didn't sound mean or bitter. Then after each time, I would rate myself on how well I had done. When I could respond with the truth about my short-lived marriage and confidently smile because I really was okay, I knew that I had reached my goal. I had taught myself to forgive.

If I could reach out to you, hold the sides of your face, and look into your eyes right now I would because I need you to get this. Whoever the person is that you need to forgive, and whatever the reason is, you cannot stay in this place. Your excuse has become a crutch for you. A crutch is something that you are supposed to use temporarily while your injured body part gets stronger. After the healing process, you can walk again without the support of the crutch. However, any time you use a crutch for too long, something happens that stunts the healing process and the injury conforms to the crutch. Instead of healing fully, you can end up healing incorrectly or stop healing altogether.

Once again, my father is a perfect example here. In Fall 2005, my father had an accident while doing what I will call extreme yard work that resulted in all of the bones breaking on his left side from his hip down to his ankle. Being seventy-five when this happened put an intense amount of stress on his body as he endured several lengthy operations to replace, reset, and reposition the bones to the right place with all kinds of weird apparatus I had never seen. Before that day, my father had only been in the hospital once, and that was as a preteen when he had to have his tonsils removed. I can speculate and say that despite the orthopedic equipment, his bones had no prior knowledge of how to heal themselves because he had not experienced injuries before.

Consequently, my dad did not seem to understand the healing process fully, either. After weeks turned into months and my father was still using a crutch to walk, it became a part of him. He now walks hunched over, and his leg appears to curve a bit outwards from the way it healed. You see, at some point during therapy, he was to challenge himself to practice walking without the crutch. This would not be something he would master in one visit to the therapist, but over a period of time and scheduled visits, he would do a little better and walk a little farther without the crutch each time. He was to do this until the point where he no longer needed it and could walk freely again. But sadly, this did not happen. Fifteen years later, my dad still walks with a crutch because at some point in that first year or so, the orthopedic surgeon and the neurologist told him that he would likely never regain feeling in the bottom of his foot, which was the reason why he could not step fully with any security. Instead of returning to his normal, healthy walk, he draws the attention of anyone he passes because of how he now walks with that crutch. What is really interesting is how much I struggle to recall how he walked before the accident, even though I saw him walk without it for the first thirty-two years of my life. His crippled walk is the only thing I remember.

I love my father with my whole heart, but this is not the segment of his life I want you to follow. Just as you gasped when you read that he is still using a crutch to walk almost fifteen years after his injury, I gasp at the thought of you using unforgiveness as a crutch for that long. If you don't recognize that it is time to put it aside and get better at forgiving, step by step, you are going to do just as my father has done and convince yourself that you will never heal. And you will live out the rest of your life hunched into a new shape that does not allow you the freedom to walk with a free spirit that only comes with a heart that forgives. And if it goes on long enough, just like I don't recall my father's former walk, people will struggle to recall how you were before you were hurt.

"If you insist on being selfish, be selfish and forgive. It's really about you anyway."

#DLynneSpeaks

TWO

WHAT YOU'RE REALLY SAYING
WHEN YOU DON'T FORGIVE

Some people are so focused on doing for other people that they often fail to prioritize themselves. If that is you, and I asked you right now to list the most important people in your life, you might easily name your spouse, child or parent before you even think to name yourself. And you would not be the only one. The number of people who put others first is as enormous as the hearts of the people themselves. But before you get caught up in how amazing it sounds to be characterized as having a big heart, I ask you this: would you consider adding the name of the person you are still angry with to that same list of people you prioritize above yourself? Probably not. Nevertheless, that is exactly what you are doing when you don't forgive; you are putting yourself last, even after the person you aren't forgiving. That person and that offense have been allowed to take precedence in your thought life, and it is you who gave him or her permission. Ironically, you may have convinced yourself that you are ignoring the person, but it is quite the opposite.

Unforgiveness positions you to give attention to the person who has done you wrong whether you want to or not, especially if the struggle to forget about it is consuming you. For example, you can be casually going about your day, and then something can trigger your thoughts about the hurtful experience. You try your best to eject the bombarding thoughts from your mind, but you realize that you don't even recall the content of the last page you just read. Or maybe you don't remember making the last three turns on your commute to work, but now you are there, and you realize that hurtful moment has been playing in your mind during the last leg of your commute. I could list countless other examples of how we "lose time" as our thought life carries us to places we are not always willing to go, but you get the point. Your unpleasant memories of the hurtful moment hijack your thoughts without notice or invitation, and the price you pay is having to go back and read the last page again or having to pause and be grateful that you made it to work safely when you were not paying attention to the road like you should have been.

What exacerbates all of this is the realization that the person with whom you were upset seemed completely unbothered. How did that make you feel? More upset, right? Who's losing here? You are. You are walking around angry about what your spouse did wrong, and your spouse is walking around carefree. You are seething, unable to think of anything other than the offense, and he's humming a tune or enjoying the game on television. His happiness is getting you angrier by the minute. Meanwhile, you are losing valuable time that could be spent doing things that you either need to get done or enjoy doing. At times, you may be physically in the same room with your family or friends, fully intending to spend quality time together—at the dinner table, at the movies, at a sporting event, or wherever—but not mentally or emotionally there at all. Instead, your mind is ruminating over the offense you endured. You are a mere prisoner of the past, and you are missing all the fun happening right in front of you. Or perhaps this was your one night of the week to have some "me time," and you are so busy thinking about the offense that your "me time" is slipping away. The preciousness of now is losing territory to the pain of your past. Unforgiveness has you prioritizing your past over your present, giving attention to someone who deserves your brain space far less than you do. Even if that person is dear to you, you still need to care more for yourself than anyone else because you are the only person who is always with you.

Since we have addressed how you can unintentionally say that the offender is more important than you are, let's also look at what may be an intentional effort to hold onto unforgiveness. Perhaps it is a power struggle. You think that not forgiving someone positions you to keep that person forever in your debt because you are not giving them something they need. Consequently, what you don't realize is that you need to forgive more than the other person needs your forgiveness. I know she hurt you, so choosing to withhold your forgiveness may seem like you are holding her fate in your hands. Here's the real dilemma, though:

how do you think it is possible to hold that person's fate without holding your own? How can you hold something in place and be somewhere else at the same time? Let's use a more tangible example to bring more clarity. Suppose you are wrestling. If you are trying to pin someone, which is to hold him in a certain position where he cannot move, once you get him into that position where you appear to have the upper hand, you have to stop and be still too. With all the strength you can gather, your main goal is to keep the person from getting free to turn things around and pin you instead. You would be foolish to expect your opponent to stay still if you decide to get up and do something else. If you look around or even sneeze, you risk loosening him to regain the freedom to get away from your grasp.

The wrestlers represent you and the person you are not forgiving. It is like you are holding someone in the same spot where the offense occurred. Whatever kind of life relationship you shared beforehand stopped at that moment. If you were walking down a sidewalk together when the offense occurred, choosing not to forgive is like stopping right there on the sidewalk and never taking another step. If you choose to part ways and walk away alone, nothing would force that person to stay there if you leave. But unforgiveness is wanting that person to stay in that spot, and your effort to limit that person's progress is limiting yours as well. It is saying we cannot go on because you hurt me, and because of what you did, this is where we stop.

I can understand why choosing not to forgive someone would make you feel powerful because when someone hurts you, you feel exactly the opposite—powerless. The situation was completely out of your control because if you had been in control, getting hurt would never have happened. That's why it's important to understand that if the person comes to you seeking forgiveness, he or she is asking for a gift from you. Having the option to say yes or no is quite powerful. The ability to bind someone, as in my previous wrestling example, is a clear demonstration of your power. You are showing your strength. But since unforgiveness is the power to bind, and forgiveness is the power to free, isn't the power to free much greater? If given a choice to stay stuck in one place or to walk about freely, would you not choose the latter?

There is a movie based on the autobiography of a boxer named Rubin "Hurricane" Carter.[2] The storyline depicts Carter's wrongful imprisonment for a crime he did not commit. Decades later, after learning about his story, one family puts all of their time, energy, and money into getting him released. They grow extremely close to Carter in this process and grow to love him as they develop a familial relationship with him over time while trying to prove his innocence. There is a scene in the film where Carter is talking to the son in the family fighting for his freedom, and he says, "Hate put me in here. Love is gonna bust me out." When he is finally proven innocent and freed, the corrupt systemic players who held him captive for decades saw their reign of power come to an end. Hate binds. Love frees. Forgiveness wins.

See how this works? Time and power or energy are probably two of the most highly sought-after intangibles we know. Yet when you choose not to forgive, you are really saying that neither of these is important to you, which I doubt is true. Two main reasons people say they are unable to do things they need or want to do are lack of time or energy to get them done. But here you are, giving away both of them. The very thing that most people wish they had more of is the very thing you are giving away because of your decision not to address your feelings at their core. This is why I need you to take a moment to ask yourself what your truth is. Are you pretending to be over something that you are suppressing, which is costing you valuable time that you cannot get back? Or are you holding on to the feeling of false control because you have the power to give the gift of forgiveness but are choosing not to release it, which is keeping you bound as well? I need you to see that it is far more costly to give up your time than it is to give your forgiveness, and likewise, it is more powerful to extend forgiveness than harbor unforgiveness. Own your truth so that you can see what message you are sending to others, and more importantly, to yourself. I am certain you can think of plenty of things that you need to accomplish that do not afford you the luxury of wasting time or energy. Now that you recognize what your truth is, let's make the needed adjustments to put you on a more productive life path.

"I OWE IT TO MYSELF TO FORGIVE AND BE FREE BECAUSE IT'S A GIFT THAT'S ALREADY BEEN GRANTED TO ME."

#DLynneSpeaks

THREE

LIVING YOUR BEST LIE: WHY YOU MUST FORGIVE

If you have not heard at least one person say the phrase, "live your best life," I don't know where you have been for the past five or so years. Oprah Winfrey herself has even made the phrase a staple in everything connected to her, from her podcasts and television network to *O Magazine*, which has a segment in each issue called "LYBL." To say it's a popular phrase is an understatement. So is saying that not everyone who claims to be doing it is being truthful. People are out here struggling to keep up the look of living their best life. I know because I was one of them. Before I reached the point when I truly forgave my ex, I was dealing with a host of other things that I just could not seem to get through. I went through what felt like interminable sadness that was followed by a period when I had convinced myself that I was finally okay. I was definitely the personification of wasted time, as explained in the previous chapter.

At first, I knew I was a mess. Initially, I spent much of my time crying, feeling empty, being angry, and questioning everything. How could he do this to me? Even worse, how could I have let this happen to me? I had moved to a place where I realized that it was impossible to blame one person for everything that happened in a relationship between two people. So now I needed to forgive two people, and that other person was me. My work had doubled. The burden of it made me tired all the time, which is what led to a series of issues. I mentioned previously that I went through a period of what I call "undiagnosed depression." The product of that depression was disrupted sleep patterns, abnormal eating, unexplained weight loss (which I would have appreciated if it weren't coupled with the other issues), isolation that led to strained friendships, and poor work habits. All of this was exacerbated by the random crying spells that hit me out of nowhere. I was losing time. I was going nowhere. At least that was how it felt. I had to figure out a way to get past this rut in my life because the physical and emotional fatigue carried me from one lie to the next. What other choice did I have? When I had to leave the house, I had to prepare myself to see people along the way. Someone was going to make the mistake of asking how I'd been, and my unrehearsed response was going to be a flood of tears that I couldn't turn off. I could not allow that to happen—at least I didn't want it to—so I had to practice lying, on cue, "I'm good," until I could escape their presence and let out all of the feelings brought on by their question. I was not built to endure that kind of life.

Ten months into my marriage, I was supposed to be living my best life, but I was living my best lie. This lie was one that *I thought* I was playing out quite well because I was always certain to keep up my outward appearance, no matter how horrible I felt inside. After all, my mother always taught me not to go anywhere ugly, so I always did my hair and put on some lip gloss, a cute outfit, and of course, that bright and shiny platinum wedding ring set, even if I was just making a quick run to the store. But who cares how cute you are if your heart is dark? In that state, I was no benefit to anyone. This wasn't at all what my mother meant for me when she taught me that. If nothing else, of that I was certain.

My moment of truth came when I confessed what I was dealing with to someone who is now a dear friend of mine, but who was someone I only knew casually at the time. She was an assistant in the department where I was a faculty member, and one day, she felt comfortable enough to whisper to me that she had applied for another job. My whispered response to her was, "Well, since we're sharing, my husband has lost his mind and my marriage is a wreck." And much to my surprise, her reply was, "Girl, mine too!" I didn't see THAT coming. But that moment of truth freed me. I would venture to say that she, too, was freed.

Telling the truth is a fundamental need of the human spirit. Maintaining a lie is exhausting. It required every ounce of what energy I had left after the bouts of crying. Part of me was freed the moment I owned up to the desolate situation I was calling life at that moment. I was finally positioned to move beyond living my best lie and move forward to forgive myself and him so I could heal. I could now use my energy to do the work of forgiveness rather than waste it on keeping up the facade that all was well. And if I was going to transition from faking smiles when people asked how I was enjoying married life to answering truthfully and disclosing that we were no longer together and that I was *truly* okay, I was going to need to get started as soon as possible. To get to the other side of unforgiveness, I needed to accept the truth and feel the anger so that I could fully deal with it and be healed.

A story of a woman named Stacy Jackson completely inspires me to do the work of forgiveness. Although she has a common name, the woman herself is likely a stranger to you because stories like hers don't always get the notoriety they deserve. She is the mother of the late Jerry Brown, Jr. of the NFL's Dallas Cowboys. He was a passenger killed in a car crash because the driver of that car was intoxicated. That driver was his good friend and teammate, Josh Brent. Now, I am not sure how far their friendship had taken them as it relates to Brent having a relationship with Brown's mother, but I can only imagine how hard it was to cope with knowing that the negligence of her son's friend cost her son his life. As if the emotional strain of losing her son was not enough, there were people who likely increased that strain by questioning her decision to allow Brent to attend the funeral. She could have easily been angry and upset by such questioning, but with forgiveness in her heart, her voice, and her actions, she answered with poise. During her interview with Eric Ray of CBS Sports, Ms. Jackson said, "What do you have to give to the rest of the family if you're bitter? So, I had no problem with him [Josh] coming to the memorial service. I had to forgive him."

She was hurting, I am certain, but she knew that holding the hurt in the form of anger and unforgiveness towards Brent would not bring back her son, nor would it make any aspect of the grief process better. It was as if she considered it bad enough that the family had suffered one loss with Brown's death. If she harbored a cold and unforgiving spirit, the family would have not only lost Brown, but they would have also lost their matriarch. It would have totally changed her. She knew this, and as a result, she said that she *had to* forgive. In her mind, there was no other option. Her future and her family's survival depended upon it.

Stacy Jackson's story is one that sets quite a high bar when it comes to forgiveness. Somehow, she managed to see past her pain to sympathize with Josh Brent, the one she needed to forgive. She had to change her perspective and see him as worth more than any image the media or her own mind could have made him out to be. I am sure that it was not easy to do, but she decided that to live the best life possible, forgiveness was necessary. Conversely, you may be thinking that the person you have not forgiven is not important enough to your well-being for you to be concerned about extending forgiveness to him. But let me assure you that just because you may not need or want that person in your life does not mean that forgiveness is unnecessary.

Forgiveness does not always need to lead to restoration of a relationship, but it does always lead to restoration of your heart. You need to be healthy again. Forgiveness is a gift that you give to another person, whether he deserves it or not, and it is also a gift that you give to yourself when you unlock the door that has been holding you hostage to your pain and blocking you from achieving success in all the areas of your life. I challenge you to own your truth and assess whether or not your future is all that you want it to be. Only you can figure out if the lie you have been telling yourself, the one that says you're alright without forgiving that person, is the one thing holding you back from living your best life.

"WHEN YOU'RE GOING THROUGH HELL,
DON'T STOP."

AUTHOR UNKNOWN

FOUR

How to Forgive

I will grant you that forgiveness is not the easiest thing to do, but not for the reasons you may think. It isn't hard because the person made you mad enough never to want to see her again. It isn't hard because he hurt you so badly that you have deemed him unworthy of your forgiveness. I will reiterate here: forgiveness is not for the other person as much as it is for you. So, what makes escaping feelings of unforgiveness so hard? You may not have a clue as to how to do it. At one point, you may have decided or told the person that you would forgive him, but when you saw him again, everything changed. All of the negative feelings rushed in, and you got angry all over again. You gave it your best shot, but it didn't work. What if it did, but you just gave up on the process too quickly?

You tried, but it didn't work. Let me clarify a common misconception about forgiving. The decision to forgive happens in an instant. The process of forgiving happens over time. Read the last two sentences again. Did you? Good. Because I need you to understand that you are not going to be over it instantly, at least not a deep hurt. There are offenses that I consider to be quite minor that I only allow myself about twenty minutes to get over, but for others, I have to go through a full-blown process to get to the point of forgiveness. This is going to sound like too much extra work, but if it helps you finally get over something you have been harboring for days, weeks, months, or even years, I would say it is worth it. So now that you see the difference in the decision versus the process, you have to make a forgiveness plan—something you can look to as a guide when you cannot rely on your feelings to force you to do what's necessary for your well-being. Ask yourself what it should look like when you have fully for-given this person. Visualize the ultimate peaceful state that could exist for you, and if you are feeling generous, include the other person too.

Take, for example, the story that Oprah Win-frey tells in her Masterclass Podcast about her au-dition for the role of Sophia in Steven Spielberg's film, *The Color Purple*. She had never acted before but had fallen in love with the novel by Alice Walk-er upon which the film was based. Consequently, she had determined, prayed, and believed that she would get the part when she auditioned be-cause there were so many signs that pointed to it. The casting director, however, was determined to make her feel otherwise. He proved this by tell-ing Ms. Winfrey that she was not a real actress and that she was no match for the renowned Al-fre Woodard, who had auditioned just before her. Crushed, she left and went through a series of thoughts about what she would do if she did not get the part. It started as a decision not to see the film, even though she adored the book and want-ed nothing more than to see the film adaptation. Then she transitioned to desires of wanting to see the film anyway, and finally to the desire to see the film anyway and be happy for Ms. Woodard. That was her moment of freedom. She envisioned herself being happy, even if the results did not turn out in her favor. She took the time to plan out her behavior to come to a place of peace.

You may say that the example of Ms. Winfrey was not one of unforgiveness, but even so, the feelings of anger and hurt were the same. What will your plan for getting to the other side of unforgiveness look like? You do not have to be formal and write it out, although that would make it much more real to you, but you can just talk it out with yourself and make decisions about how your behavior will change. Start with small goals and build on them. Perhaps, in the beginning, you will be able to mention the person's name without your heart skipping a beat. Or maybe you can see him walking towards you with his new fiancée and be genuinely cordial to both of them even though it didn't work out for the two of you. Who knows? You may even be able to get over the fact that he snubbed you out of the promotion and still offer to pick up both of your sons from school and take them to football practice because you know he now has to work late. Plan out whatever you decide that it should look like and do whatever you need to do to make it happen. If you have to go as far as talking to yourself or posting reminders that read, "I will smile when I see him next time" or "I will offer to take his son to practice," carry it all the way out. The combination of visualizing what it looks like and establishing a plan of action to do it makes what may have seemed to be a daunting task now seem somewhat more palatable.

Stop replaying the offense in your mind. I know you think you can't help it, but you can. You have to figure out how to stop it the same way you get that song you don't like out of your head because it came on the radio during your morning commute. Continuing to sing it may be a subconscious behavior in which you keep catching yourself, but you have to press the button and change the station. In this case, changing the station of that mental replay means you have to find something else to think about. If you followed my suggestion from the previous section and created a plan of what complete forgiveness looks like, you already have something handy that can serve as your replacement therapy. I have to emphasize this because replaying the scene is not healthy for you, so you must treat it like a bad habit that you need to break to save your life. It's just that serious.

Take smoking or drinking, for example. I am not using this to pick on anyone who engages in either. This is just an example to which many people can relate. I have heard former smokers and drinkers who did these things habitually say that the hardest part of quitting was the need to have something in their hands or just finding something to do instead of lighting up or taking a drink when the urge hit. Similarly, when you find yourself replaying the scene that hurt you, take a moment to acknowledge that it is happening...again. When you catch it happening, you may need to say to yourself audibly, "Hey. Cut it out." Follow that up with talking out your plan—operation replacement therapy. It doesn't matter what you have to do. Get to the other side.

There are several reasons why you have to stop yourself from replaying the hurtful scene. First, you will start to change the details the more it happens. Maybe it's just me, but I promise you that I have never been able to tell a story the exact same way each time unless I am reading it. When I taught high school, I had three class periods of American Literature. Even using my lesson plan prompts each time, I never could manage to say the same thing each time, even though I wanted to be sure each class was getting the information I wanted them all to have. At the end of the day, I would still cringe at the thought of the things I forgot to tell one class versus the other. In the same way, you can retell yourself the story so many times, but in your case, the truth can get distorted. You may even visualize yourself as more of a victim than you actually were. Ironically, in my situation with my ex, I knew I was healing because I started to recall fewer details. But if you are replaying the scene and become more of a victim each time, you are going in the opposite direction of healing. The hurt worsens and your ability to forgive decreases. And just as I mentioned that I knew I was healing because I recalled fewer details, if you keep replaying the story and do not notice that your response to it is less raw or hurtful, you have work to do. You want to be able to talk about it without feeling the pain or anger that you once associated with it. That is where your true freedom lies.

Don't be stupid. When someone apologizes for doing something minor, such as bumping into you, for some reason, the automatic response is, "It's okay." This response is not one that we give much thought, but if someone took it literally, it could be completely misinterpreted. I remember hearing a comedian telling a joke about using a public restroom in a stall with a malfunctioning lock. She described the scenario of a woman hovering over the commode, trying to handle her business while unaware that the stall door is not locked properly. In bursts another woman in a frantic search for an empty stall, and the two lock eyes for a brief, yet extremely awkward millisecond.

Woman who bursts in: "Oh! Sorry!"

Woman using the bathroom: "Oh! It's okay!"

Woman who bursts in: (Calls to others) "Hey ladies, come on. Over here. She says it's okay!"

Of course, the audience bursts into laughter at the mere thought of how ridiculous that would be. We all know that although she said it was okay, that is not what she really meant. In that case, saying "it's okay" means I forgive the mishap. It does not mean that you are welcoming another opportunity to experience it again.

The same goes for when you forgive someone of a hurt that is far more serious. Extending forgiveness to someone does not mean that it was okay that she did it, nor does it mean that you position yourself to let it happen again. It means that we are going to move forward as though this did not happen so that we can both be okay again. That is the goal of forgiveness. We have to seek to restore ourselves and the person being forgiven to a place where we can both move forward and live free of any pain that was caused, whether you are the person who caused it or the one who was hurt by it.

At times, saying "it's okay" and moving forward on separate paths is necessary. There is no rule stating that once you decide to let go of unforgiveness, you have to maintain a relationship with the person. Forgiveness does not always equal reconciliation. Not everyone is meant to be in our lives for our entire lives, so if that season is over, then it is acceptable to let go and move on without remorse for doing so. This is especially true if you notice that the person's behavior patterns are too much a part of her core being to expect that she won't hurt you again—possibly in the same way. You are going to have to use wisdom. I have had relationships that came to a hurtful end that forced me to evaluate whether or not trying to restore them was the best thing for my future. Sometimes the value added is worth the work of restoration, and sometimes it isn't.

Remind yourself of who the real beneficiary is. Most of us have been taught at some point to be givers rather than to behave selfishly as takers. But taking does not automatically mean you are selfish, and when it comes to getting to the other side of unforgiveness, the process allows you to be both a giver and a taker at the same time. If you are scratching your head and asking how that is possible, allow me to remind you of what I have said many times already. Forgiveness is not about the other person as much as it is about you. This is an effort to focus on getting you back to your healthy state of mind, body, and spirit so that you can succeed in the things that you want, unhindered by a force that seemed out of your control until now. Moreover, this is your chance to do something for yourself that not only helps you, but it also helps everyone else connected to you. Your personal freedom positions you to make a greater impact on the people connected to you, whether or not the person you have forgiven is one of them or not.

Remember, I stated previously that unforgiveness puts the attention on someone else when you are actually the one who deserves the majority of your attention. Forgiveness is you putting the oxygen mask on yourself first before assisting someone else in an airplane that is losing cabin pressure. It is germane to your survival.

Recognize that you have needed it and will need it again. Have you ever done something that you came to regret? Don't get deep on me and start giving answers that imply you live a life of no regrets because even though you made mistakes, you learned from them all. That kind of response avoids this question. Whether or not you learned from your mistake, it may be safe to say that everyone above the age of four—and trust that I avoid grand generalizations, but I am saying everyone this time—has made at least one choice in life that did not yield the results you wanted. Therefore, it is also likely that someone else may have been affected in some way by your decision. To go a bit further, the effect may not have been something the person liked. This means that at least once in your life, you had to apologize to someone for something you did. For this reason alone, you should forgive whoever it is that you have not yet forgiven. And no, it does not matter that what you did was minor in comparison to what this person did to you. The conditions of extending forgiveness are not predicated on what the offense was, but on what it is that *you* need for yourself. Whether you believe in "what goes around comes around" or "you reap what you sow," the bottom line is that since you wanted to be forgiven for any wrong you have done, intentionally or uninten-tionally, you have to forgive others.

"EACH TIME YOU AVOID THE OPPORTUNITY TO CONFRONT AND WORK TO RESOLVE THE PAIN OF YOUR PAST, YOU WILLINGLY HAND OVER TO THE DEVIL EVEN MORE TIME THAN WHAT HE HAS ALREADY STOLEN FROM YOU."

#DLynneSpeaks

FIVE

TIME IS NOT YOUR FRIEND

Every time I hear someone say, "Time heals all wounds," I want to scream, "NO IT DOESN'T!" I swear, people must say this because they feel pressured to avoid a silent or awkward moment, but in this case, silence truly would be golden. Now, if you are one of the people who makes a habit of saying this, keep reading. This is not the time to tune out. I need you to allow me to challenge your thoughts on this so that you can use time to your benefit instead of just treating it as some arbitrary intangible with mystical healing powers. Time is powerless. Time cannot do anything for you other than pass you by. Everything that happens during the process of time passing is a byproduct of some other effort. Getting to the other side of unforgiveness is no different. You have to decide to do the work...and then do it.

Let me be clear. When it comes to tragedy and dealing with the pains of life that hurt us deeply, I am the first person to say that you cannot allow anyone to tell you what you should be feeling and how long you should feel that way. I am not negating that here. Instead, I am saying that going on indefinitely, waiting to feel better just because you are "giving it time" is building your hopes on something false.

Have you ever watched a talk show or interview of some kind where a person is talking to someone about something hurtful that happened years or even decades ago? The person can be conversing normally with the psychologist or interviewer and even laughing, until all of a sudden, his memory of some awful moment in his life is jarred by a question or comment that comes up during the discussion. And then the tears. And I don't mean soft, sentimental tears that seem only to show a vague memory of what happened, but deep, visceral tears that seem to be full of present-day pain that involves his entire being. If time were the heal-er so many have proclaimed it to be, what is the precise amount of time that it takes for humans to get over past hurts? Is there a chart somewhere with a list of specific pains and how long it takes to get over them? If so, who determines these pa-rameters? No one. It is not something anyone can calculate because it is up to the individual to do something with the passing of time to heal, and the sooner that happens, the better.

Going through that break up with my ex put me through a pain that I had never experienced before. My misery was almost indescribable, but I am thankful for a circle of friends who saw through the smoke and mirrors and came to see about me. One friend came to pick me up one day and took me to New York City to go shopping for some new clothes because she knew that my self-image was completely wrecked at that point and she wanted me to see that I was still beautiful. She would not allow me to sit around moping and being angry about my situation at that time, and she insisted that doing so would only prolong my ability to be happy and find love again.

If you want to stay sad and stuck, a surefire way to do that is to sit alone and think about how you have been wronged. The upside-down days in which I had been merely existing before that heroic shopping trip could have easily continued had I had refused to go. I could have stayed home, replaying any one of the dreaded scenes that marked the end of my marriage. I could have dwelled on the constant reminders of my dwindling self-worth. I could have stayed angry about how my life was falling apart. I could have remained bitter and full of blame towards my soon-to-be-ex and kept wasting energy and time on something I had the power to change. I could have. But if I had continued to let them replay in my mind, time was sure to work against me, and the facts were bound to get jumbled as my emotions led me to add and leave out details of what had actually happened. After all, the average human mind can barely hold onto information accurately for a few moments before details get twisted. At this point, several months later, details were not becoming clearer. Time was only making things worse.

Take this far less traumatic example, for instance. When I started my career, I had the misfortune of finding myself in a situation for which I was not fully prepared. I was new and unaware of all that should have been involved or asked before accepting one of the jobs I had to do. But in my delusional commitment to provide some kind of meaningful input to the assignment, I stayed until the end. I fumbled through the roughest few hours of my professional life and finally left, certain that I had done horribly and feeling troubled about the whole thing. I must have called a colleague to vent or something because I recall talking to him shortly after that. This seasoned colleague stopped me amid my lament and said, "You got twenty minutes to get yourself together and move on." That still guides me when I encounter tough moments.

The thought of how I have some tough friends is quite laughable as well. But I am grateful for tough friendships and my ability to transfer that skill to other areas of my life. Every time something happens to me that is hurtful and full of potential to steal an entire day away from me when it barely deserves twenty minutes, I check myself. One day, I saw something that read, "Did you have a bad day, or did you have a bad few minutes that you milked for a whole day?" This captures my point exactly because often we allow things to linger on and steal time away from us that we can never get back. When you sit back and let time heal the wound, it gets infected instead.

You can stop the infection. Set a limit for yourself to feel whatever it is that you feel about what happened to you but have a cut-off point. I am not saying it has to be twenty minutes. Just set a limit that is less time than you typically take to recuperate from hurt, if for no other reason than the fact that you have decided that you don't want to be miserable any longer than you can help it. If needed, think about how being stuck in the space in time when the infraction happened keeps you from being present for all the other things that happen until you finally let it go. The argument with your spouse or your child on the way to work has you upset and unable to focus on the presentation you have to give to the directors at 10:00 AM. The thing your co-worker said to you that was a tad disrespectful has you seething, and you miss the big play your child just made at the game after school because your mind was wandering instead of being fully engaged, supportive, and present in the moment that counts more.

Stop hanging out with time like it's your bestie who can help you feel better. Time is not your friend. In fact, time will have you convinced that you no longer need to forgive your real friend or whomever it is that has you upset. Time will lie to you and have you telling yourself that you have made it this far without forgiving the person, so getting to the other side of unforgiveness is no longer critical to your well-being. Lies. You need to cross over. You need to get to the other side. Everything important to you is waiting on the other side. The longer you wait, the shorter the time you have to focus on and enjoy what is most important to you.

Meanwhile, sitting over on this side of unforgiveness with Time, your new bestie, is adding to your list of regrets without you even realizing it. Just like anything else worthwhile, forgiveness must be intentional. Regrets are accidental. And no one dies wishing they had stayed angry with someone a little longer than they did. In fact, most people who do decide to put aside unforgiveness probably wish they had done it sooner. I know I do. The unhealthy loss of weight, hair, self-esteem, and most of all, peace of mind, were not worth the time I lost before I decided to forgive my ex and myself.

"Forgiveness is connected to your total life's well-being. It's possible. It's necessary. And it's already yours."

#DLynneSpeaks

Conclusion

From the Bottom to the Top

I love to see people healthy, happy and enjoying life as much as possible and for as long as possible. When I see people hurting, it grieves me. It makes me wish I could figure out how to hug them and take away their pain. As a believer in God, I know that is not my role, but I do believe that He uses me to facilitate this in my sphere of influence. Consequently, when I see people hurting from something they think is beyond their control when it is really something over which they have far more power than they perceive, I am annoyed and almost indignant.

Indulge me for just a little longer. One of the most annoying things to me is when a fly somehow gets in my house. Because I often sit in complete silence at home, the sudden buzz of a fly zipping by my ear gets my attention with little effort. Immediately distracted from whatever I am doing, catching the pest becomes the focus of more of my attention than something so small truly deserves. My method of capture used to be more of a struggle but is now automatic. I used to stand in the middle of the room and try to follow the pest with my eyes to watch for its landing, which could have been anywhere. This was exhausting, but I finally noticed that it always went for the artificial light or the window, I guess because the light seemed like a way out. I got clever, and now I reduce the sources of light to as few as possible to limit the places where the fly will be drawn. Then I stand completely still, swatter in hand, waiting to hear or see where in which of those places it lands. Once it gets to a place where the light is, I move in a stealth-like manner to approach it and allow it time to get comfortable enough to stop flying about furiously. And then, SWAT! It's over. I usually get it on the first try, but that is because I have developed a method and somewhat perfected it. It used to take much longer and require many more swats, but now I do this far more easily.

I need you to consider unforgiveness as if it were that fly. Just as the fly is a distraction, the state of being in unforgiveness is also a distraction to the full life that you are intended to live. In the beginning, unforgiveness will catch you off guard because you will think you are going about everything in your life in a normal way, unaware that it exists. It may not be noticeable at first, but it's there. When you do finally realize its presence in your life, you will spend more of your time dealing with it than you really want to. There will be things you are trying to do but cannot do successfully because now that you realize unforgiveness is living in your heart, it will stay in your subconscious mind as something you will eventually need to deal with, even though you may decide not to move or swat it out of your life right away.

On the other hand, you may exert a full effort to rid your life of unforgiveness by taking a swat at it, and you may even be convinced that you killed it. But just like that fly, unforgiveness knows how to play dead or disappear into some mysterious place after you swat at it, and it will resurface just when you are about to get on with your life. Be persistent. Persevere. You will squash this whole thing for good if you don't quit. You are bigger than it is. Being annoying and occasionally hard to locate are the only strengths unforgiveness has, but the more you work at being good at dealing with such a nuisance, the easier it will be to annihilate each time. Eventually, you will be skilled at this because you will know how to bring it to the light so that you can deal with it directly. Once you understand this, unforgiveness cannot continue to distract you from your life's purpose. You will be able to focus and get rid of it once and for all. This is the level of focus that accelerates you to your destiny. This is what empowers you to go get what's yours!

One key thing to realize is that it is acceptable to be disappointed with someone without being unforgiving. Work diligently to manage your feelings about the disappointment rather than allowing your feelings to manage you. Ultimately, the goal is to avoid a situation where you look back on your life and wish that you had wasted less time being powerless to unforgiveness. Now, here's what I need you to promise yourself. Don't let this be a book that you read and don't apply. Take time to go back and revisit the parts of the book that made you the most uncomfortable and walk through the discomfort by giving yourself time to practice the concept before revisiting another section. If you have been holding on to a moment in time that hurt you or made you angry, realize it has been holding you back in some way since the day it happened. Depending on how long ago it happened, that may also mean that the forgiveness process will take longer. But you can declare your independence now.

Of course, I am not expecting you to be able to say that the healing is complete by the time you finish reading this. I just need you to remember that it all starts with a decision. Once you decide that YOU ARE WORTH IT, the rest becomes a manifestation of what your worth looks like. Eliminate the excuses you have been using to remain unforgiving. Come to grips with the fact that you are making the offender a priority over yourself when you choose unforgiveness rather than forgiveness. Stop believing you have dealt with the situation if anytime you think about it or discuss it, you still relive all of the emotions that you experienced when it happened. And most of all, don't talk yourself out of believing that forgiving is possible *for you*. Make a commitment to pay close attention to who you are and figure out what it will take for you to practice forgiving more each day. Having a prepared response and setting reminders to make positive affirmations that supported my goals worked for me, but you may need to think of something different to do. But hey, if you can't think of another approach, try mine. When you start somewhere, it positions you to see how to make adjustments that better suit your style.

A few years ago, I realized that some people are absolutely horrible at apologizing. At the same time, I concluded that no matter how horrible people are at apologizing, I was going to be stellar at forgiving. This is how I maintain my own peace. While my belief in God allows me to pray and release my problems to Him, the release, and therefore, my peace, is my responsibility. They will attain their peace from their own efforts to pursue it. That being said, years later, my ex apologized for all that he had put me through. He also told me that he wanted to do right by me as an honor to his dad, who had always loved me. My ex and I had both come a long way from what felt like the bottom of an abyss of darkness and hurt. And while I vividly recalled making that early-morning call from my car to summons him to come out of that woman's house, it didn't grieve me. In fact, I even discussed it with him and was able to talk about it as if it had happened to someone other than me because I had long since forgiven him. And while I assured him of forgiveness as well, I also mentioned that it was nice to get both the apology and sincere remorse from him. But if the apology had never happened, I still would have been the one responsible for making sure that I came to my own place of reckoning...my place of solace...the other side of unforgiveness. I needed that more than anything. I deserved it. So do you.

ENDNOTES

1. Apostle Michael A. Freeman is the pastor and founder of Spirit of Faith Christian Center. See www.mikefreemanministries.com for more information about how you can hear him live or online.

2. *The Hurricane* is a motion picture distributed by Universal Pictures, released in December 1999.

3. *Oprah's Masterclass Podcast, Part 2,* Oprah Winfrey.

About the Author

Danita Lynne is an educator and sign language interpreter who is passionate about language and equal access to language for all. She is Founder and CEO of English and Sign Language Masters, LLC (ESLM) where her award-winning service as an advocate, instructor, and an interpreter bridge the language gap between individuals who are hearing and deaf/hard-of-hearing, especially where both groups share educational, professional, or even familial environments. Additionally, under ESLM's umbrella of services, Danita works with public figures and authors as an editor and proofreader for print and electronic media projects, a natural transition she made after teaching high school and college English composition for more than ten years.

FOLLOW DANITA LYNNE

Facebook -

English & Sign Language Masters, LLC - ESLM

Instagram -

@DLynneSpeaks

PRACTICAL STEPS TO OVERCOMING PERSONAL HURT

Use the following open-ended statements to guide you in your personal journey to getting to *The Other Side of Unforgiveness*.

Note that there is not a size requirement for the hurtful situation that comes to mind. You deserve to be free from EVERY offense, whether small or large so you can be limitless in EVERY area of your life.

1. After having read this book, the person I need to forgive most is...

_____

_____

_____

_____

_____

_____

_____

2. The concept mentioned in *The Other Side of Unforgiveness* that made me realize how I am still harboring unforgiveness against this person is...

_____

_____

_____

_____

_____

_____

_____

_____

_____

_____

_____

_____

_____

_____

_____

_____

3. Of the seven reasons listed in Chapter One: Why You Can't Forgive, I most identify with reason #_____ because...

_____

_____

_____

_____

_____

_____

_____

_____

_____

_____

_____

_____

_____

_____

_____

_____

_____

_____

4. I am now determined to get to *The Other Side of Unforgiveness* concerning the person I named above. That means that when I see or talk about this person, I don't want to feel hurt or angry, but instead, I envision myself being able to...

_____

_____

_____

_____

_____

_____

_____

_____

_____

_____

_____

_____

_____

_____

5. In order to achieve the desired feeling I just described, three things I can do IMMEDIATE-LY to get me closer to making this vision my new reality are...

_____

_____

_____

_____

_____

_____

_____

_____

_____

_____

_____

_____

_____

_____

_____

_____

_____

Made in the USA
Middletown, DE
06 September 2019